HEAL the HURT
that
RUNS your LIFE

Other Books by Bill Ferguson

How to Heal a Painful Relationship
And If Necessary, How To Part As Friends

Miracles are Guaranteed
*A Step-by-Step Guide to Restoring Love, Being Free,
And Creating A Life That Works*

Audio Cassettes

Heal the Hurt That Runs Your Life

How to Love Yourself

How to Have Love in Your Life

How to be Free of Guilt and Resentment

How to be Free of Upset and Stress

How to Create a Life That Works

How to Create Prosperity

How to Find Your Purpose

How to Experience Your Spirituality

Spirituality: Teachings from a World Beyond

How to Divorce as Friends

HEAL the HURT
that
RUNS your LIFE

BILL FERGUSON

Return to the Heart
P.O. Box 541813
Houston, TX 77254

http://www.billferguson.com

Return to the Heart
P.O. Box 541813
Houston, Texas 77254
U.S.A.
(713) 520-5370

Cover design by Mark Gelotte

Edited by Michele Hegler

Library of Congress
Catalog Card Number: 96-92380

ISBN 1-878410-21-0

Made in the United States of America

CONTENTS

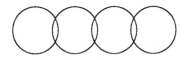

CHAPTER 1

SET YOURSELF FREE

When you were a young child, you were pure love. You were happy, alive and free. Just look at little children. This love, freedom and aliveness is the essence of who you are. This is your natural state. This is the way you started.

Unfortunately, you were born into a world that suppresses this state. Instead of being born into a world that is loving and supportive, you were born into a world that is critical and harsh.

Sooner or later, you got hurt. You experienced invalidation, rejection and painful losses of love. You experienced this hurt from your parents, your friends and the world around you.

As a little child, the only way you could explain this loss of love was to blame yourself. Obviously you were the problem. In a moment of hurt, you decided that you were worthless, not good enough, not worth loving, a failure, or in some other way, not okay.

This wasn't the truth, but this became your truth. This was the only explanation that made any sense at the time. You then hated the very notion that you created. "No one can ever love me if I'm worthless. Worthless is a horrible way to be."

The moment you bought the notion that you were not okay, and started resisting this notion, you created an internal mechanism that would then sabotage the rest of your life. From that moment on, the underlying focus of your life would be to avoid this hurt.

A good way to see this hurt is to notice what happens the moment you get upset. Notice the immediate and powerful surge of feelings and emotion that come forth. This is the hurt that runs your life.

You may never notice this hurt, but it is

certainly there. It determines your actions and shapes your life.

In a subconscious attempt to avoid this hurt, you set in motion a process that destroys love and creates a life of fear, upset and suffering. Here is how it works.

Whenever something comes along that reactivates this hurt, you feel threatened. Then, in an instinctive attempt to avoid this hurt, you fight and resist your circumstances.

This automatic fighting and resisting then creates a state of fear and upset that destroys your effectiveness and almost always makes your situation worse.

When you get upset, you close down inside. You lose your creativity and your ability to see clearly. You get tunnel vision and you interact in a way that destroys love and creates opposition and resistance against yourself.

Upsets seem to be caused by what happens, but they're not. Upsets are caused by your fighting and resisting what happens. To see this in your life, pick a recent upset.

Now go to the moment the upset began.

Didn't something happen? Didn't that circumstance happen whether you liked it or not? Of course. No matter how upset you got, that circumstance was still there.

Now notice what would happen to the upset if somehow you were at peace with what happened. There would be no upset.

This is because the upset wasn't caused by what happened. The upset was caused by your fighting and resisting what happened. When you take away the resisting, the upset disappears.

No circumstance has the power to cause an upset. Circumstances can only reactivate suppressed hurt that is already there.

This is why the same thing can happen to two people and one person will get upset and the other won't. Different people get upset at different circumstances because each person has a different set of suppressed hurt.

Now notice that the same type of upset keeps showing up in your life. The same upset keeps showing up because the same hurt keeps getting reactivated.

This hurt also creates the same type of

problems in your life. Notice that no matter what you do, there are certain areas of your life that never seem to work. This is because these areas of life reactivate your hurt.

To avoid this hurt, you fight and resist. This then creates a state of fear and upset that destroys your creativity and keeps you from seeing what you need to do. You then interact in a way that keeps this area of your life from working. You also create more hurt.

For example, Mary had the hurt of feeling unlovable. To avoid her hurt, she needed a relationship. She needed someone to tell her how lovable she was.

In her eagerness to find someone, she could never wait for the person who was best for her. She would settle for anyone who was half-way acceptable. As a result, none of her relationships worked.

Even if she found someone who was perfect for her, she would soon destroy the relationship. She would get upset over and over because the other person wouldn't give her enough love and attention. Her fear and upset would then push the person away.

Then she would hang on to the person.

She would hang on because, if the person left, she would have to face all her hurt of feeling unlovable. By her hanging on, she would push the person even further away.

Eventually, all her relationships would leave. Mary did everything she could to be lovable, but everything she did to avoid her hurt created more of it.

The same thing happens with every one of us. The specifics are different, but the process is the same.

Every one of us has a hurt that we run from. For one person, the hurt is failure. For another, the hurt is not good enough. For another, the hurt is something else.

Every one of us has a very specific hurt that runs our life. The avoidance of this hurt is what sabotages our lives.

To be free inside and to be effective in life, you need to discover what your hurt is and be free of it.

Basically, the cause of your hurt is some issue you have with yourself. You bought the notion that in some specific way, you were not okay. Fighting this notion is what creates your hurt. Once you take away the fighting, the notion disappears and so does the hurt.

Once you heal your hurt, your whole life begins to change. Instead of creating a life of fear and upset, you create a life of love. You restore the happiness, the freedom and the aliveness that you once had. You see life clearly and you become very effective.

The process for finding and healing your hurt is very simple and very fast. This book will show you how. All you need is the desire to be free.

ACTION TO TAKE

◆ Select a recent upset. Notice that the upset wasn't caused by what happened. The upset was caused by your fighting what happened. If you were at peace with what happened, there would be no upset.

◆ Whenever you get upset, what you are really fighting is the hurt that gets reactivated by what happens. See if you can find the hurt that's under your upsets.

◆ Notice what happens when you get upset. What happens to your peace of mind and your ability to see clearly? What happens to your effectiveness? Notice the negative things that happen when you get upset. Notice how your fear and upset sabotage you.

◆ Would you like to be free of the hurt that runs your life? You can. The healing process is very simple. Use this book to show you how.

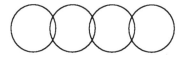

CHAPTER 2

CREATE THE EXPERIENCE OF LOVE

We all want to be happy, but we are convinced that happiness comes from outside of ourselves. We believe that happiness is determined by what we have and by what happens around us.

We then go through life trying to force life to be a certain way. We think this will bring us the happiness that we seek, but it never does. In fact, the more you try to force life to make you happy, the more you create a life of fear and upset, and the more unhappy you become.

Happiness can never come from anything outside of yourself. Happiness can only come from within.

When you are full of joy, where is the joy located? Is the joy outside of you, or is the joy inside? Obviously, the joy is inside. When you are upset, where is your upset? Inside you.

Both happiness and upsets are on the inside because this is where you experience life.

At any moment, you are having certain body sensations, thoughts, feelings and emotion. These combine to give you a very specific experience of life. This experience of life is what determines the quality of your life.

When you are experiencing love, joy and inner peace, the quality of your life is great. When you are experiencing fear and upset, the quality of your life is not so great. Notice what feelings and emotion you are experiencing right now.

We think that the experience of life is determined by what happens outside of us, but it's not. Your experience of life is determined by how you relate to what happens.

For example, have you ever had a time when the circumstances of your life were a mess, but on the inside, you were happy and at peace? Have you ever had a time when the circumstances of your life were fine, but on the inside, you were full of fear or upset?

Some people are very wealthy, but their lives are full of pain and suffering. Others are very poor and very happy.

The circumstances of your life don't determine how you experience life. Your circumstances only trigger certain internal mechanisms. These mechanisms then produce certain feelings and emotion that make up your experience of life.

Mastery of life begins when you discover the mechanisms that sabotage you. As you dismantle these mechanisms, you become able to experience life in a way that is supportive. You become free inside and able to live in the experience of love.

Ultimately, this experience of love is the happiness that you seek.

When this is present, you are free inside. You are happy and alive. You feel good about yourself and good about life. You are creative and full of energy. Life is magic and great things happen.

Look at the times of your life that you consider to have been the very best. These are the times when you lived in this state.

So what creates the experience of love? Is it communication? Openness? Trust? All of these are valuable, but none are the answer. The experience of love is created by giving the gift of acceptance and appreciation.

Notice how you feel inside when you are accepting and appreciative. Doesn't this feel good? Of course. You are at peace and full of love. You also interact in a way that enables life to work for you instead of against you.

Notice how you feel when someone genuinely accepts and appreciates you. Don't you feel better about yourself and better about life? Don't you also feel better about the person who accepts you? Don't you automatically return the love?

As you give the gift of acceptance, acceptance comes right back. This is true in your relationships and in every aspect of life.

If you look, any area of your life that works great will be an area where you are full of acceptance and appreciation. To create the experience of love and to have life work for you instead of against you, you need to be accepting.

Unfortunately, acceptance is usually much easier said than done. Some people and some areas of life are very difficult to accept. Fortunately, non-acceptance is an illusion.

To better understand the illusion of non-acceptance, find someone in your life who is difficult to accept. Now take a good look at this person. Doesn't this person have a very particular state of mind and a very particular way of behaving?

Now look a little further. Isn't this person exactly the way he or she is? Isn't the person this way without any regard for how you feel about it?

You can hate the way this person is or you can love the way this person is. How you feel about the person is totally irrelevant. This person is still the way he or she is.

This is also true about your life. At any moment, your life is exactly the way it is. The people in your life are exactly the way they are and you are the way you are.

Pick any aspect of your life that you don't

like. Notice that this aspect of your life is exactly the way it is.

Your demands and expectations for how life should be have nothing to do with the way life is. No matter how upset you get, your life is still the way it is.

Acceptance is nothing more than surrendering to the truth.

When you are at peace with the truth, you remain free inside. You see your situation clearly and you see what needs to be done. You can then interact in a way that naturally creates the experience of love.

When you fight the truth, you destroy the experience of love. You get upset and close down. You can't see what needs to be done and you interact in a way that creates opposition and resistance against yourself.

Resisting is an illusion that doesn't change a thing except inside you. Resisting only destroys the quality of life and makes your situation much more difficult.

To live in the experience of love and to be effective in life, you need to be able to flow with life. You need to let go of your demands and expectations for how life should be, and make peace with the way life is.

Let go. Then take whatever action you need to have your life be great.

ACTION TO TAKE

◆ When you get upset, notice where the upset is located. Is the upset over in the circumstances or is it inside you? Both happiness and upsets are inside you because this is where you experience life.

◆ How you experience life determines the quality of your life. Notice how you feel inside when you are full of acceptance and appreciation. Notice how you feel when you are full of fear or upset.

◆ At any moment, your life is exactly the way that it is. The people in your life are the way they are, and you are the way you are. Look in your life and see if this isn't true.

◆ Notice what happens when you fight the way life is. Notice the fear and upset that gets created. Now notice what happens when you flow with the way life is. Which way allows you to be more effective? Which creates a greater quality of life?

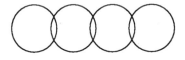

CHAPTER 3

LET GO

A lady named JoAnne was about to lose her job. She was so afraid of making a mistake and getting fired that she lived in a constant state of fear and upset. She made mistakes everywhere.

I told her that in order to keep her job, she had to be willing to lose it. When I said this, she got very upset. "What do you mean, lose my job? I'm a single mom with four kids. I can't make ends meet with a job. What am I going to do without one?" She left in tears.

When she came back the next day, JoAnne seemed like a different person. She was very relaxed and at peace.

When I asked what happened, she said that after our earlier conversation she went home and cried. She cried for hours. Then she realized that even if she lost her job, she would be fine.

"I've been through tough times before and I've made it through all of them. If I lose my job, I don't know what I'll do; but I know that somehow I'll be fine."

In her willingness to lose her job, JoAnne set herself free. She later reported that with her fear gone, she was able to produce ten times as much with one-tenth the effort. By being willing to lose her job, she was able to keep it.

Without realizing it, JoAnne did something called letting go. She let go of her demands and expectations for how life should be. She stopped fighting her circumstances and became willing for anything to happen.

The moment she did this, all of her fear and upset disappeared. She restored both her peace of mind and her effectiveness.

Letting go is the inner action that releases fear and upset.

The moment you let go, everything seems to change. With the fear and upset gone, you see your situation very differently. You become creative and discover solutions you could never have seen before. You become naturally effective.

To let go, you need to be willing for your life to be however it is. You do this by granting permission. "I am willing to lose my job." "I give you full permission to be the way that you are." "I am willing to lose you."

You don't have to like your situation, just give it permission to be the way it is and the way it may become. Let go of your demands and expectations for how you believe life should be and make peace with the way your life is. Set yourself free inside. Then take whatever action is necessary to handle your situation.

Keep in mind that letting go is a state of mind and has nothing to do with your actions. Letting go is what removes the fear and upset so you can see what action you need to take.

To make the process of letting go a little easier, there are a couple of steps you can take. The first step is trusting. Trust that no matter what happens, you will be okay.

This doesn't necessarily mean that life will turn out the way you want. Life often doesn't. Trust is knowing that however life turns out, you will be fine.

When you know that you will be fine, letting go becomes relatively easy. You can then let go, you restore your effectiveness, and life works out great. This then reinforces the trust.

When you don't trust, letting go becomes very difficult. You fight, resist and hang on. You then make everything worse, which reinforces "don't trust."

Trust is actually a choice. Trust is something you create. It's a declaration. "I will be okay no matter what happens. I trust, just because I say so."

Trust is also telling the truth. You really will be fine no matter what happens. Life is only threatening when you resist.

Look at your life. Have you ever had a situation that you didn't survive? Of course not. You have survived everything. The times in your life that you considered tough only seemed that way because you were resisting.

So stop resisting and trust. Trust that no matter what happens, you will be fine.

The second step in the process of letting go is to be willing to feel your hurt. Be willing to experience all the hurt and the feelings of being not okay that your circumstances reactivate.

The avoidance of this hurt is what makes you resist. Once you are willing to feel this hurt, the need to resist disappears. You can then let go.

For example, Robert had a fear of losing his wife, Jan. To make sure she didn't leave, he hung on to her. This hanging on then pushed her further and further away.

Robert was afraid of losing Jan because if she left him, this would reactivate all his hurt of feeling not worth loving. To avoid this hurt, he hung on.

Once he realized this, and once he became willing to feel his hurt, the loss of Jan ceased to be a threat. He no longer needed to hang on and was able to let her go.

The moment Robert let Jan go, he changed the way he related to her. Instantly, he started appreciating her. Once he knew that she could leave at any time, every second he had with her became a joy.

Instead of needing her, he started treasuring her. Jan then felt so loved and so able to be herself around Robert, she didn't want to go anywhere.

This is what happens in life. The more you are able to let go and flow with life, the more life takes care of itself.

You may not always get what you want, but you can always be free inside. You can restore both your peace of mind and your effectiveness.

The key to being able to flow with life is to heal your hurt.

ACTION TO TAKE

◆ Recall a time in your life when you let go. Remember how free you felt? Remember what a relief this was? Notice how much more effective you are when you let go.

◆ Be willing in your heart for anything to happen, but in your actions, do whatever you need to have your life be great.

◆ Trust that no matter what happens, you will be okay. When you know that you will be okay, letting go becomes much easier.

◆ If letting go is difficult, find the hurt and the feelings of not okay that you are avoiding. The avoidance of this hurt is why you resist. Once you are willing to feel this hurt, the need to resist disappears.

◆ Be willing to have nothing. The more you are willing to have nothing, the more you appreciate everything that you have.

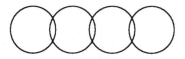

CHAPTER 4

HEAL THE HURT

When you were born, you were created with the natural ability to heal hurt. Look at little children. Little children are masters at healing hurt.

When a child feels hurt, the child cries. Then, after the child finishes crying, the hurt is all gone.

Little children are able to release their hurt because they do something we don't notice. They allow their hurt. They are totally willing to feel all their feelings and emotions.

This is the natural process for releasing hurt. Hurt is just a feeling. When you allow the feeling to take its course, the feeling quickly comes and goes.

Unfortunately, we have been taught to do the opposite. Instead of allowing our hurt, we have been taught to fight it. "Big boys and girls don't cry. If you want something to cry about, I'll give you something to cry about."

You soon learn to avoid your hurt. This then circumvents the natural healing process. Instead of allowing the feelings and letting them go, you fight the feelings and keep them inside.

You try to push the hurt away, but you can't. The hurt isn't outside of you, it's inside. So, in your attempt to push the hurt away, you actually push it deeper inside. You then spend the rest of your life running from this suppressed hurt.

The irony is that no matter what you do to avoid your hurt, you can't get away from it. You will continue to experience these feelings whether you like it or not.

When you're hurt, you're hurt. You don't have a choice whether you are going to feel it. You will. Your only choice is this: Are you going to allow your hurt like a child, or are you going to fight your hurt and keep it inside?

If you allow the hurt, the feelings disappear. If you fight the hurt, the feelings turn into pain and then stay.

To see this in your life, find a time when you were hurt and you allowed yourself to cry. Then, after you cried your last tear, you felt a wonderful freedom. This was a time when you had allowed your hurt.

Now find a time when you were hurt and hated it. You hated your circumstances and you hated your hurt. Notice that this hurt was very painful and seemed to stay forever.

The key to releasing your hurt is to be willing to experience it. Keep telling yourself, "It's okay to feel the hurt. It's okay." Let the hurt come and let the hurt go. Cry if you can.

If the hurt doesn't release, there is something inside that you are fighting. You are fighting the feelings of being worthless, not good enough, not worth loving, a failure or some other form of being not okay.

This is the hurt that you've been fighting since you were a child.

By fighting these feelings of being not okay, you created an internal mechanism that not only destroys your effectiveness, but also makes it very difficult to heal your hurt.

The hurt becomes more difficult to heal because now the hurt is no longer just a feeling. Now the hurt is a threat.

"If I'm a failure, that means that something is the matter with me. I won't be loved and my life will be painful. I can't be a failure; I must be a success."

The avoidance of this threat is what keeps us from flowing with life. It sabotages relationships, prosperity, health and every other aspect of life.

Several years ago, I saw this avoidance mechanism being created. I was shopping in a local department store when a little girl spilled her soft drink.

Apparently, the girl's mother was quite embarrassed. She became very upset and started screaming at the little girl, "What's the matter with you?" she yelled. "Why are you so stupid?"

The little girl then experienced a very

painful loss of love and started crying. She cried and cried, and she did something that changed her life. She bought the notion that she was stupid.

Clearly this wasn't the truth, but to the little girl, this was the absolute truth. What else could she conclude? "My mom knows everything and she says I'm stupid. Clearly this must be true. Besides, I did spill my drink."

The little girl couldn't help but believe that she is stupid. This is especially true if she hears this over and over.

Imagine how painful this must be. The girl started out being free and alive, full of love and joy. Then she discovered that something was terribly wrong with her. She was stupid. The hurt of this realization would have been unconfrontable.

The little girl then took the process one step further. She decided that stupid is a horrible way to be.

"No one can ever love someone who's stupid. Just look at my mom. My very own mom doesn't love me anymore, because I'm stupid. My only chance of ever being loved is to somehow become smart."

This is the beginning of the end. From this moment on, the little girl will never again be able to be herself. She can't be herself because she thinks that the way she is, isn't okay. She thinks that down deep, she's stupid.

To the little girl, her only chance of ever being okay and her only chance of ever being loved, is to be smart.

She will then spend enormous amounts of energy and effort running from stupid trying to become smart; but no matter what she does, she will never get away from stupid.

To make matters worse, anytime something hints that she's stupid, she will feel threatened and become full of fear and upset.

To avoid this threat, she will automatically fight and resist her circumstances. This then keeps her from seeing what needs to be done and has her create a life of ineffectiveness and more hurt.

The same thing happens in various degrees to every one of us. The circumstances are different but the result is always the same. Every one of us buys the notion that in some way, we are not okay.

Without ever knowing, we then go through life avoiding this hurt and sabotaging our lives. To heal this hurt and to create a life that works, you need to make peace with the feelings of being not okay.

ACTION TO TAKE

◆ See if you can find the feelings of not okay that you've been avoiding. Look at the times you've been hurt and find what those circumstances say about you. Do they say that you are a failure, not good enough, worthless or not worth loving?

◆ Remember that not okay is just a notion that you created in the moment of a hurt. It isn't the truth. However, in your hurt, it is the truth.

◆ Be willing to feel your hurt and the feelings of being not okay. Keep telling yourself, "It's okay to feel the hurt. It's okay." Let the hurt come and let the hurt go. Cry if you can.

◆ Notice that you don't have a choice about whether you are going to feel your hurt. You will. Your only choice is to allow your hurt and let it go, or fight your hurt and keep it inside.

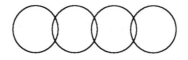

CHAPTER 5

NO JUDGMENT IS REAL

Look at the chair you are sitting on. Is the chair good enough? One person would say, "Yes, of course, the chair works fine." Another person would have a very different opinion about the same chair. "No, it's not good enough. The chair is the wrong color and the wrong shape. I don't want it."

Two people have very different opinions about the same chair. For one person, the chair is good enough. For another, it's not. Both are valid points of view, but what is the truth? Is the chair good enough or not?

Although both points of view are very valid, neither is the truth. The chair just is, and nothing more. This is the truth. Any judgment or point of view you have about the chair is just your opinion, something you add to the truth. A judgment is only one way of looking at something, a point of view.

Is your chair worth loving? One person would say, "No, of course not, how can you love a chair?" Another person would say, "Yes, everything on the planet is worth loving."

Is the chair smart or stupid? One person would say that the chair is the ultimate of stupid. A quantum physicist could say that all the intelligence of the universe is in the chair.

No matter what point of view you have about something, someone else can have a very different point of view about the same thing.

Judgments seem to be real, but they are not.

You will never be able to find a good enough, a worthy, a failure or a stupid. You can perceive something as worthy, but you can never find a worthy.

Judgments don't exist in the physical universe. They only exist as thoughts, as points of view.

When someone buys the notion that he or she is worthless, not good enough or not okay, this is just a point of view. This is never the truth.

However, to the little girl who bought the notion that she was stupid, this is much more than a point of view. This is the absolute truth. "No one can ever love someone who is stupid. In order to be loved, you have to be smart." To the girl, both smart and stupid are very real.

The moment the little girl bought the notion that she was stupid, she created a mental standard called smart/stupid. She then grows up judging herself and others by these opposite points of view. "This person is smart. That one is stupid. I'm smart. I'm stupid."

She doesn't notice that she is judging. She thinks that she is observing the truth, but she's not. She is observing her truth.

When she looks at herself through the point of view called smart, every cell in her body will seem smart. When she looks at herself from the point of view called stupid, the very core of her being will seem stupid.

To the little girl, both judgments are very real. One moment she will experience herself as smart. In the next moment, something will happen and she will experience herself as stupid. Both are present all the time.

Now here is where we get into trouble.

Both aspects are present all the time but our culture teaches us that this is impossible. You can't possibly be both smart and stupid at the same time. You must either be one or the other. You must either be smart or stupid, worthy or worthless, lovable or unlovable.

We have been taught that you can't be both, but in reality, you can't be either. Judgments aren't physical objects. They are points of view, and in this realm, you can't be just one. You must be both.

Smart and stupid come together in the same package. You can't have one without the other. Each point of view is necessary for the other to exist.

Likewise, you can't have big without small, up without down, left without right. The same is true for any judgment. You can't have good without bad, worthy without worthless, success without failure. You must be both.

Unfortunately, we never notice that we're both. We are convinced that we can only be one. We are also convinced that in order to be okay, you must be the one considered positive. You can never be the one considered negative.

You can't be a failure, you must be a success. You can't be worthless, you must be worthy. To be a failure or worthless would be a horrible way to be.

Now this creates a serious problem because you can't be just one. You must be both. You are both worthy and worthless. You are also good and bad, lovable and unlovable, adequate and inadequate, strong and weak. All of these are aspects of being human.

When you believe that part of who you are shouldn't be there, you set yourself up for some very serious suffering.

You lose your ability to be human. You sabotage your confidence and your love for yourself. You lose your ability to flow with life, and you push away the happiness that you seek.

You put yourself under tremendous pressure to become a certain way, but no matter what you do, you can never get there. You can never get there because the place you are trying to get to doesn't exist.

There is no place in the universe where you can have success without failure, worthy without worthless. They all come together in the same package. You may experience worthy from time to time, but as long as you resist worthless, worthless will keep showing up.

You can never overcome the aspects that you resist. Everything you do to get rid of them makes them stronger. However, you can stop fighting them and make peace with them. As you do this, they lose their power and disappear.

ACTION TO TAKE

◆ Look in your life and see if you can find a worthless or a not good enough. Notice that you can't. Judgments aren't physical objects. They are only points of view.

◆ If you have the hurt of stupid, you will see life in terms of smart and stupid. If you have an issue with failure, you will see life in terms of success and failure. What are the standards by which you view life?

◆ Notice that in your reality, both sides of the standard are very real. Sometimes you will experience yourself as one aspect, sometimes the other.

◆ Notice that much of your life has been spent trying to get rid of one side of the standard and only having the other. Do you see how impossible this is? Do you see how much you have suffered trying to accomplish something that can't be accomplished?

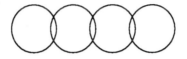

CHAPTER 6

MAKE PEACE WITH YOURSELF

What are the aspects of you that you've been resisting? Look for the word or words that hurt the most. Are you worthless, not good enough, not worth loving, a failure or some other form of not okay?

Once you get a rough idea of what your issue is, notice that being this way has never caused you any trouble. All the trouble has been caused by what you've done to avoid feeling this way. The trouble has been caused by your fighting, resisting and hanging on.

Not okay has never caused you any trouble because not okay doesn't exist. Not okay is just a thought. Only the resisting is real.

By resisting the thought of being not okay, you give your issue power. Here is a short exercise that can demonstrate this.

Imagine two large yellow balloons on the ceiling above you, but don't think about them. Whatever you do, don't think about those large yellow balloons on the ceiling above you. You just thought about them. Don't do that. Stop.

Notice what happens when you try not to think about the balloons. You keep thinking about them. In fact, you can hardly think about anything else. Your resisting keeps the thought alive.

The same is true with the feelings of being stupid, worthless, not good enough or whatever your issue is. Ultimately, these feelings are only a thought. By your resisting the thought of being this way, you give the thought power. You also keep your hurt from healing.

To heal your hurt and to set yourself free inside, you need to stop the resisting. You do this by accepting and embracing the aspects of you that you've been avoiding.

Although these aspects don't exist in

reality, they do exist in your reality. To you, they are as real as the chair you're sitting on. You have just been avoiding and denying them.

Once you let in the fact that these aspects are there, that these are aspects of you, the resisting stops. The aspects then lose their power and disappear.

I learned this the hard way.

Most of my life was spent running from failure. This was an aspect of myself that I did not want to face. I would do anything to avoid experiencing this hurt.

In my drive to become a success, I would overspend and take unreasonable financial risks. I created a life of fear and upset. I lost my ability to see clearly, and I acted in a way that produced more and more failure.

Finally, I failed so big I was forced to face this aspect of myself. I lost everything. I lost my property, my office and even my home. Failure was in my face like never before.

This was by far the most painful time of my life. Failure was everywhere. My entire life seemed to be one big failure. The evidence was overwhelming.

I was forced to let in what I had feared the most. I was a failure. I could no longer avoid or deny it. Success was also an aspect of me, but at the time, all I could see was failure.

As I let in what a failure I was, something shifted inside of me. My fear of failure lost its power. How can you run from something that's always there no matter what you do? Running from failure is like running from your shadow. You can't.

I didn't know it at the time, but I had just made peace with failure.

I was sad for a while, but soon my whole outlook seemed to change. The fear and upset that ran my life had disappeared. I no longer had to be a success. I could just be me.

This was an incredible relief. I hadn't been able to be me since I was four years old. I thought that in order to be okay, I had to be a success. I never dreamed that this was just a notion that I had made up. I never dreamed that it was okay to just be me.

This new freedom produced a very subtle yet profound change in the way I lived my life.

Instead of running from failure, I was able to put my focus on discovering what works in life.

When I ran from failure, I couldn't see what worked. In fact, what worked was irrelevant. "Don't bother me with what works. I'm not interested. Tell me how to avoid failure. I'm interested in that."

By running from failure, I lost my effectiveness. I sabotaged my dreams, and I created more failure.

Once I made peace with this aspect of myself, there was nothing left to fear. Both success and failure lost their power. I could then put my focus on creating a simple life that works. I stopped overspending and I got out of debt.

I continued to go for my dreams, but I did so in a way that was effective. As time went on, my dreams began to come true. Now I have a life that I could never have imagined.

My life turned around the day I made peace with failure.

What are the aspects of you that you have been avoiding?

ACTION TO TAKE

◆ The aspects you've been resisting don't exist in the physical universe, but they do exist in your universe. Notice how real they are to you.

◆ Notice that these aspects have never caused you any trouble. They are only thoughts. All the trouble has been caused by the things you've done to avoid feeling this way.

◆ Look at your life and notice how much you avoid the feelings of being worthless, a failure, or whatever your issue is. Notice how much these feelings keep showing up in your life.

◆ Notice how much you have sabotaged your life running from the hurt of not okay trying to become okay. See if you have suffered enough. Are you now willing to make peace with this aspect of you?

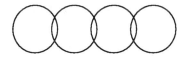

CHAPTER 7

START THE HEALING PROCESS

You now have the opportunity to discover and heal the issues that have been sabotaging your life. You can experience a freedom that you haven't had in years. The process isn't difficult, but you need some diligence.

You can read the next few chapters quickly and understand how the process works, but the mere understanding won't change the way you live your life.

To change your life, you need to make a shift on the inside. You need to experience the truth of this in your heart. Work through these next few chapters as if your life depends on it. It does.

First, we'll go over the basic steps in the healing process. Then we'll show you how to find your issue and how to heal it.

1. Find the issue that runs your life.

You create your issue by fighting some aspect of you. The first step in the healing process is to discover what that aspect is.

When you discover what your issue is, you won't like it. Just the thought that you may be this way is enough to send cold chills up and down your spine.

To discover your issue, find the aspects that you hate the most. Are you worthless, not good enough, not worth loving, a failure or some other characteristic?

Find the word or words that create the most discomfort. The more painful the words, the stronger the issue.

While you are looking, pay special attention to any aspects that you may be denying. "I know I'm not worthless." "I am definitely not a failure."

If you are certain that you are not a

particular way, this will be an aspect of you that you are resisting. You wouldn't be defensive unless you had something to be defensive about. To be free of your issue, you may need to see something about yourself that you don't want to see.

Keep looking for the word or words that are the most painful. We'll talk more about this later.

2. Be willing to experience all the hurt of being this way.

We resist certain aspects of ourselves because we don't want to feel the hurt that these aspects reactivate. Once you are willing to feel this hurt, you no longer need to resist.

To the extent you are unwilling to feel your hurt, you will be forced to resist. You won't be able to make peace with these aspects, and you won't be able to heal your hurt.

To be willing, all you need to do is make a choice. "Yes, I am willing to feel all my hurt. I'm scared, but I'm willing."

Remember, hurt is only a feeling, an emotion. Separate yourself from your circumstances and allow yourself to feel whatever feelings are there. Keep telling yourself, "It's okay. It's okay."

The moment you become willing to experience your hurt, you stop resisting your hurt. The aspects you've been fighting then cease to be a threat. You can then make peace with them and let them go.

3. Look at your life and see that you are this way.

To be free of your issue, you need to stop the resisting. To do this, you need to do the opposite of resisting. You need to make peace with these aspects. You need to accept them and own them.

The best way to do this is to look in your life and see that these aspects are there. You are worthless, not good enough, a failure and so on. You are also worthy, good enough, and successful, but you aren't fighting these aspects.

Look for the aspects that you've been fighting. Find the evidence to prove that they are there. There will be plenty of proof if you are willing to see.

As you let in the fact that you actually are worthless and so on, these aspects lose their power. Only in the denial and resisting can the aspects exist. When you take away the denial and resisting, the aspects disappear.

Notice that some of these aspects may already be losing their power. This is because you are beginning to make peace with them.

4. Know that being this way doesn't mean a thing.

As you discover that you are this way, you soon discover that being this way is irrelevant.

"I'm a failure. So what? I'm also a success. What does failure have to do with tomorrow? Absolutely nothing. I can still do what works. I can still go for my dreams, and I can still have a great life."

You will be free of your issue when you know that the aspects you've been resisting are part of you, and that having them doesn't mean a thing.

ACTION TO TAKE

◆ Make sure you take the time to walk through the healing process. Merely reading the chapters is not enough to change your life. To change your life, you need to work the chapters.

◆ Create within yourself a commitment and a determination to do whatever it takes to discover and heal the hurt that runs your life.

◆ Walk through the process on a feeling level rather than a conceptual level. Stay in touch with your hurt and work to release it.

◆ Remember that being not okay doesn't mean a thing. You are also okay.

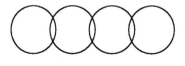

CHAPTER 8

FIND YOUR ISSUE

The first step in the healing process is to discover what your issue is. What are the aspects of you that you hate the most?

Use this chapter to discover what those aspects are. When you find an aspect, ask yourself this question. "How do you feel at the notion that you are this way?" If the thought of being this way is particularly painful, you are getting close to your issue.

Keep looking for the word or words that hurt the most.

Which of these aspects do you avoid?

To start the healing process, look over the following list of common issues. If possible, have someone read them to you. Hearing an issue is much more reactivating than reading one.

Listen to each word as though it accurately describes who you are. Then make a note of the words that reactivate the most hurt.

How do you feel at the notion that you are the following?:

unlovable	useless
not wanted	a nothing
not needed	unimportant
not worth loving	don't matter
worthless	a nobody
no good	a loser
not good enough	a failure
don't measure up	can't cut it
not enough	don't have what
not good enough	it takes
to be loved	incompetent
inadequate	screwed up
insufficient	something is wrong
less than	with you

stupid	self-centered
unstable	inconsiderate
inferior	selfish
defective	dishonest
weak	bad
helpless	wrong
needy	evil
clingy	heartless
a wimp	ugly
a coward	fat
irresponsible	a slut
unreliable	just like your
lazy	parents

Notice that some of these aspects are painful and some aren't. The aspects that aren't painful are ones you don't have an issue with. Look for the ones that hurt.

What are your upsets?

One of the best ways to find your issue is to look at your upsets. This is true because every time you get upset, one of your issues has just been reactivated.

Some circumstance has triggered the hurt of feeling worthless, not good enough, failure or some other form of not okay. Resisting this hurt is what creates your upset.

Make a list of every major upset and every major hurt you can think of. Be sure to include the upsets that keep repeating themselves in your life.

Be as specific as you can. What happened? You don't need a detailed explanation. Just say enough to remind you of the incident. See if you can come up with at least fifteen different times when you got hurt or upset.

Once you complete your list, use the following steps to discover the issue that's under each upset.

◆ Go to the moment the upset began. What happened? What was the specific circumstance that triggered your upset?

◆ Now go to the hurt that's under your upset. Actually feel this hurt if you can.

◆ In this hurt, you will find an aspect of you that you don't want to experience. What is it? What do your circumstances say about you?

◆ Find the word or words that hurt the most.

As you do the exercise, remember that you are not looking for the truth, you are looking for the hurt. In truth, the circumstances don't say a thing about you, but in the hurt, they say a lot.

If someone leaves you, this could say that you are not worth loving. If you lose your job, this could say that you are a failure. For each upset, find what the circumstances say about you.

As you work with your list of upsets, you will discover that the same aspects keep showing up. Make a note of these aspects and keep looking for ones that are even more painful.

How is your relationship with your parents?

Another area to look for your issue is in your relationship with your parents. This is especially true if you have a lot of hurt from your relationship. A good look at this hurt can reveal the aspects that you have been running from.

Go back in time and allow yourself to feel this hurt. What did your parents imply about you in their actions and in their words? Did they say that you are worthless or not good enough?

Don't look for the truth; look for the hurt. Your parents may have never felt this way about you, but in your hurt, you believed that they did. In your hurt, what did your parents say about you?

How do you feel when you are with them today? What do they reactivate in you now? How do you feel at the notion that everything your parents said or implied about you was the truth? You really are this way.

If this is a painful thought or if you say that this isn't true, you may have found the hurt that runs your life.

Make a note of the aspects and keep looking.

What do you resist in your parents?

How do you feel at the notion that you are

exactly like your parents? For most of us, this is a very uncomfortable thought. If this is uncomfortable for you, you may have found your issue.

If you hate certain aspects of your parents, you will hate these aspects wherever they show up. You will hate them in other people, and you will hate them in yourself.

What are the aspects that you hate? List each one of them. Each one will be an aspect of you that you are resisting.

You may not do the same things that your parents do, but this doesn't mean that the aspects aren't there. Notice how much you strive to be the opposite. You wouldn't try to be the opposite unless you were trying to get away from something.

Once you see that you are just like your parents, your resistance toward them disappears. You can then treat them with love and compassion.

Are you certain that you are not this way?

Every aspect that exists is in each of us. If there is an aspect that you deny having, this will be an aspect that you are resisting. This is especially true if you can see that you are the opposite. "I am a success. I am not a failure."

Success is an aspect of you, but this is only one side of the coin. In order to have success, you must also have failure. You can't have one without the other.

Also, you wouldn't be defensive about this aspect unless you had something to be defensive about. If someone said you were an eight-foot blond, this wouldn't bother you at all. If someone said you were a failure, or whatever your issue is, this would strike a nerve. This wouldn't strike a nerve unless there was a nerve in you to be struck.

We deny these aspects so we don't have to feel the hurt. If you discovered that you really are this way, you would have to face all the hurt that you've been running from. Avoiding this hurt is what sabotages your life.

To set yourself free, you need to face your hurt. This may be uncomfortable, but this may be one of the most important things you can do in your entire life.

What are your fears?

Fears are very similar to upsets. The main difference is that in a fear, you are avoiding a future event. In an upset, you are avoiding a past or present event. Both fear and upsets are created by avoiding the hurt of some issue.

If you have a fear of losing someone, what you really fear is all the hurt that would be reactivated if the person left. You would have to experience the hurt of feeling not good enough or not worth loving. Avoiding this hurt is what creates your fear.

Make a list of all your fears. Be as specific as possible. Then walk through the following steps. Do this for each fear.

◆ Find the specific event that you fear.

◆ Put yourself in the fear. Experience all the feelings and emotion that are being reactivated. Look for the aspects that you are avoiding.

◆ If your fear comes true, what would you have to experience? What would those circumstances say about you?

◆ Find the word or words that hurt the most.

Do you have a fear of rejection or abandonment?

The fears of rejection and abandonment are very common. If you have one of these fears, this will be a sign of a deeper issue. The real issue will be some aspect of you that is being reactivated.

Would an incredibly wonderful, magnificent person be rejected or abandoned? No way. Not according to us. So what kind of person would this happen to? This would happen to someone who is clearly less than wonderful.

What would it say about you if you were rejected or abandoned? What aspects of you would you have to face? For most people the hurt is being unlovable or not worth loving.

What are the standards by which you judge?

Each of us has a different set of standards by which we judge. These standards seem to be universal but they are not. Each person has a different set of standards, and each standard is created by an issue.

Remember the little girl who bought the notion that she was stupid? The moment she did this, she decided that stupid was a horrible way to be. She decided that in order to be okay, you need to be smart.

She now judges herself and others by the standard of smart and stupid. She respects people she judges as smart, and she resists people she judges as stupid.

The standards by which you judge will reveal your issues. Any characteristic you can't stand in another person is an aspect of you that you are not at peace with.

What are the standards by which you judge? What aspects do you consider to be important and what aspects do you consider to be horrible? What do you hate in other people?

Make a list of every negative aspect by which you judge. Then go down the list and for each aspect, notice that you are this way. If the thought of being this way is un-comfortable, you have found another aspect that you are resisting. Keep looking.

What are you driven toward?

Each of us are driven to escape the aspects we consider horrible and to become the aspects we think we should be.

If you have an issue with worthless, you will be driven to become worthy. If you have an issue with failure, you will be driven to become a success.

By discovering what you are driven toward, you can discover what you are driven from. One way to do this is to discover what you need for your happiness.

Actually, you don't need anything outside of you to be happy. Happiness can only come from within, but when you have these issues, there seems to be certain things that you need.

What do you "need" for your happiness? Do you need money? Do you need to have a loving relationship?

Find what you need to be happy. Then look at the opposite. What would you have to experience if you could never have what you feel you need? What would those circumstances say about you?

For example, if you never have enough money to pay your bills, this could say that you are a failure. If you never have a loving relationship, this could say that you are not worth loving.

What aspects would you have to experience if you could never have what you "need" for your happiness?

Here is another way of looking at the same thing.

Have you ever had times in your life when you took three steps forward and then got knocked back five? Where were you trying to get to? Three steps forward, toward what? Five steps backward, toward what?

The three steps forward seem to take us closer to the happiness we seek. The five steps backward bring us closer to the issue we are running from. Where are you trying to get to and what are you running from?

Find what you are driven toward. Then look at the opposite to discover what you are driven from. These are the aspects that you avoid.

What is your issue?

Now go back and review the list of common issues. See if any new words stand out. Then look over the chapter and find the aspects that show up over and over. This is the hurt that runs your life.

You may have one primary hurt that keeps showing up or you may have several. For example, you may have the hurt of failure and also the hurt of not worth loving. Select the one that hurts the most.

Then find the words that most accurately describe this hurt. Be as specific as possible. To be more descriptive, you may want to use a combination of words. You may want to use combinations like: worthless failure, hopelessly unlovable, stupid loser, or weak, whiny wimp. Find the words that are the most reactivating.

You can work with all the aspects later, but for now, find the one that does the most damage. Once you find the words that describe this hurt, you are ready for the next step.

ACTION TO TAKE

◆ Use this chapter to find the aspects of you that you've been resisting. Find the word or words that hurt the most.

◆ The best place to find your issue is in the hurt that's under your upsets. Move to your hurt. Then ask yourself, what do your circumstances say about you?

◆ Keep asking yourself this question: "How do you feel at the notion that you are this way?" If this is a painful thought, you have found an aspect of you that you are not at peace with.

◆ Pay special attention to any aspect that you deny having. You wouldn't need to deny an aspect unless you had an issue with it.

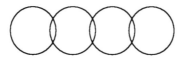

CHAPTER 9

RELEASE YOUR ISSUE

The next step in the healing process is to make peace with the aspects of you that you've been resisting. As you do this, you heal your hurt. The aspects lose their power and you become free.

The following questions will walk you through a discovery process that can make this happen.

To be most effective, get in touch with your hurt before you start the exercise. Recall the specific aspect that you are going to work with and then ask yourself, "How do you feel at the notion that you really are this way?"

Use this question to reactivate your hurt. Then start answering the questions. Take your time and allow yourself to experience the truth of each answer. Work with each question until you can say "yes."

♦ Notice how you feel at the notion that you are this way. Is this a painful thought?

♦ Notice the tremendous amount of hurt associated with being this way. Is this a hurt that you have not wanted to experience?

♦ Do you see that you would do almost anything to avoid this hurt?

♦ Is this a hurt that you have had to experience over and over again whether you have wanted to or not?

♦ Are you willing to be free of this hurt?

♦ Are you now willing to experience all the hurt of being this way?

Notice that you don't have a choice. You are going to feel this hurt. Your only choice is this: Are you going to allow yourself to feel the hurt like a child, and let the hurt go, or are you going to fight the hurt and keep it?

Allow yourself to experience all the hurt of your issue. Cry if you can. Crying is the most powerful way to release your hurt. Do this now if you can.

◆ Can you create within yourself the desire to look for and find even more of this hurt so that you can release it as well?

The more you look for the hurt, the more the hurt disappears.

◆ Do you see a lifetime of incidents where you have felt this hurt? Find as many incidents as you can.

◆ Wasn't each time you felt this hurt more proof that down deep, you really are this way?

◆ Are you willing to discover that this is the

truth? You are this way.

◆ Do you see a lifetime of evidence to prove that this is true?

This is the most important part of the healing process. To the extent you know that you are this way, your issue disappears. Search for evidence to prove that this is an aspect of you.

Look at all the times when you felt the hurt of being this way. Each time will be more proof. Let in the fact that you are this way and allow yourself to feel your hurt.

This is one aspect of you. There are thousands of aspects of you, but this is certainly one of them.

◆ Is it obvious that you are this way?

◆ Is this an aspect of you whether you like it or not?

◆ Is this an aspect of you even if you hate it and deny it?

◆ Is this an aspect of you that you have been fighting most of your life?

◆ Do you see how much you have suffered trying to avoid, deny and resist this aspect?

◆ After all you've gone through to get rid of this aspect, do you see that the aspect is still there?

◆ Are you willing to stop fighting this aspect and make peace with it? Are you willing to surrender to the truth?

◆ Do you now give this aspect full permission to be there? Isn't this aspect going to be there anyway?

◆ Do you now give this aspect full permission to be there forever and ever, to never go away?

◆ Find the aspect that is opposite of the one you've been resisting. For example, worthy is the opposite of worthless. Do you see that much of your life has been spent running from your hurt, trying to become this opposite?

◆ Do you see how much you have suffered and sacrificed, trying to become this opposite? Do you see how much you have sabotaged your life?

◆ Do you see the enormous pressure you have put on yourself, having to be the opposite of your issue?

◆ After all you've done to get from worthless to worthy, or whatever your issue is, do you see that you haven't gotten there yet? Do you see that you never can?

No matter what you do to become worthy, worthless will keep showing up. Worthy and worthless are always side by side. Trying to become worthy without worthless is like chasing a rainbow. You can never get there.

◆ Can you imagine the relief and the freedom you would experience if you never had to be the opposite, if you could just be you?

You haven't been able to be you since you bought the notion that you weren't okay. From that moment on, you had to be a certain way. You put an enormous burden on yourself.

◆ Are you willing to give up forever having to be the opposite?

◆ Are you willing to give it up forever and just be you?

◆ Do you feel a difference inside? Do you experience more freedom and peace?

Continue to feel the hurt of your issue and keep looking for more and more evidence to prove that you really are this way.

To the extent you know that this is an aspect of you, resisting this aspect becomes impossible. Your issue then loses power and quickly disappears.

Take the time to do this exercise with every aspect that you've been resisting.

Keep in mind that being a certain way

doesn't mean a thing. "I'm this way. So what? I'm also the opposite. What does this have to do with tomorrow? Nothing. I can still do what works, and I can still have a great life."

After you've finished, tell a friend all the aspects of you that you've been resisting. This will allow you to own these aspects even more.

ACTION TO TAKE

◆ Use the questions in this chapter to make peace with the aspects of you that you've been resisting. Take your time and allow yourself to experience the truth of each answer.

◆ Be willing to feel your hurt and look for evidence to prove that you are this way. This is the most important part of the healing process.

◆ Keep in mind that being this way is irrelevant. It doesn't mean a thing. You are also the opposite.

◆ Do this exercise with every aspect of you that you've been resisting. Use the opportunity to become totally at peace with every aspect of you.

◆ Tell a friend all the aspects of you that you've been resisting.

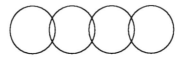

CHAPTER 10

USE YOUR UPSETS FOR MORE HEALING

Notice that the aspects you've been resisting no longer have the same power. Notice that they never will. By owning and accepting these aspects, you have taken away the resistance that keeps them in place.

To the extent you know that you are a particular way, that aspect will permanently disappear from your life. If you have owned 60% of an aspect, 60% will be gone forever.

To the extent you haven't owned an aspect, that aspect will come back. It will never come back with the same power and force as before, but it will definitely come back. It will come back in the form of an upset.

The opportunity is to use each upset for more healing. Use your upsets to show you the aspects of you that you are not at peace with. Then make peace with them.

Take the following steps whenever you get upset:

◆ Find the specific circumstances that you are upset about. What happened?

◆ Notice that your being upset doesn't change a thing.

◆ Separate yourself from the circumstances. Notice that what's going on in your life is not the cause of what's going on inside of you.

◆ Find the hurt that is being reactivated. Allow yourself to feel this hurt. Cry if you can.

◆ Ask yourself these questions. "Why can't I be at peace with what happened? What do those circumstances say about me?"

◆ Find the aspects that you are resisting and let in the hurt of being this way. "I'm a worthless failure. I hate it but I can't deny it. This is definitely an aspect of me."

◆ Keep in mind that being this way doesn't mean a thing. "I'm a failure. So what? I'm also a success."

Every time you see a little more of what you've been resisting, a little more disappears. Eventually, there will be nothing left. You will be able to laugh at your issue and feel the relief of no longer having to be a certain way.

Go through life looking for aspects that you are not at peace with. Then make peace with them.

If you ever find an aspect that is particularly difficult to accept, look for your fear. What do you fear will happen if you let in that you are that way?

Do you fear that by accepting this aspect, you will become even more this way? This is a common fear but has nothing to do with the truth. If anything, the opposite is true. You become more this way by resisting.

Also, accepting an aspect doesn't mean that you go through life saying, "I'm worthless. I'm worthless." Accepting an aspect is saying, "I'm human. I'm human." Allow yourself to be human. Then do whatever you need to have your life be great.

Until you make peace with every aspect of you, you will never make peace with life. This is because life will forever reactivate the aspects of you that you are not at peace with.

You will continue to fight and resist any circumstance that reactivates this hurt, and you will continue to create a life of fear, upset and suffering.

As you make peace with yourself, you restore your ability to flow with life. You remain creative and effective. You see life clearly and can see what you need to do.

Making peace with yourself is the key to creating a life that works and the key to having your dreams come true.

ACTION TO TAKE

◆ Notice that the aspects you've been resisting no longer have the same power. Notice that they never will. This is because you have started owning and accepting them.

◆ Use your upsets to reveal new aspects that you've been resisting and to discover deeper levels of old ones.

◆ Each time you get upset, move to the hurt and find what your circumstances say about you. Then let in the hurt of being that way.

◆ Look for areas of life where you can't flow. Then use the steps in this chapter to set yourself free inside. Get to the point where you are willing for anything to happen.

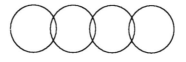

CHAPTER 11

BE FREE OF ALL GUILT

To make peace with yourself, you need to make peace with the aspects of you that you've been resisting. You also need to make peace with your wrongdoings. In other words, you need to be free of guilt.

The key to releasing guilt is to recognize that we all go through life doing the best we can with the extremely limited equipment that we have. Unfortunately, what we have is seldom enough. As a result, we make mistakes. Sometimes we make big ones.

Making mistakes is part of the human process. This is how we learn. Every time you make a mistake you discover a little bit more about life. You then become a little wiser and more aware. If you look, the most valuable lessons you've ever learned are those that you learned the hard way.

Everyone makes mistakes. What matters is what you do with them. If you recognize that you did the best you could with where you were at the time, you remain free inside and able to get on with your life.

When you condemn yourself, you lose your confidence and self-respect. How can you possibly feel good about yourself when your guilt says that you are a horrible person?

Guilt also reinforces the feelings of being not okay. This then keeps your hurt in place and keeps you from flowing with life. You feel undeserving and hold yourself back.

To have your life be as great as it can possibly be, you need to be free of all guilt.

The first step in releasing a guilt is to have the desire. Since you are the one that created your guilt, you are the one that needs to let it go.

Guilt is self-inflicted. We create guilt to punish ourselves. We think that if we punish ourselves enough, this will somehow make up for what we did. We are our own judge and jury.

Maybe now you have suffered enough. Ask yourself, are you willing to be forgiven? Are you willing to be free of your guilt? Have you been punished enough?

If not, go get a big stick and beat yourself some more. Beat yourself until you feel sufficiently punished for what you have done. Then forgive yourself.

Take a moment and make a list of everything you have ever done that you feel guilty about. Then select a specific incident that you would like to be free of. Use the following questions to release your guilt.

◆ Did you do that thing for which you have guilt? Face what you did and allow yourself to feel your hurt.

◆ Now go back in time to the moment you did whatever you did. At that moment, didn't you have a very particular state of mind? Didn't you see life in a very particular way?

◆ Didn't you act totally consistent with that state of mind and the way you saw life at that moment?

◆ If you knew then what you know today, if you had a different state of mind, wouldn't you have been able to interact very differently?

◆ You didn't know then what you know today, did you? You didn't have a different state of mind. You only had what you had, and that wasn't enough.

Five years from now you will be much wiser and more aware than you are today. However, the wisdom you are going to have in five years doesn't do you any good today. Today, you only have the wisdom that you have.

Likewise, your wisdom of today didn't do you any good back then. Back then, you only knew what you knew at the time. If you had today's wisdom, you could have operated very differently, but you didn't. You only knew what you knew.

"But I should have known." Nonsense.

How could you possibly have known more than you did? Even if you think you did know, you didn't know enough to change your actions. You certainly didn't know the consequences like you do now.

If you look, you did the very best you could with the very limited equipment that you had. If you had a different state of mind, you would have been able to handle your situation very differently, but you didn't. You only had what you had.

◆ Didn't you do the very best you could with the limited equipment that you had?

◆ Are you willing to experience all the hurt from what you did?

One of the main reasons we have guilt is so we don't have to feel this hurt. Once you are willing to feel this hurt, you no longer need your guilt. Cry if you can.

You can forgive yourself and still be sad. You can also regret what you did. You just don't need to beat yourself up anymore.

◆ Are you willing to forgive yourself for not knowing, for not being wiser and more aware? You might as well.

◆ Are you willing to forgive yourself for acting consistent with your limited awareness?

◆ Are you willing to forgive yourself for the damage you caused as a result of your not knowing?

◆ Do you now totally forgive yourself for not being wiser and more aware, and for doing whatever you did? Do you now let go of all guilt for your actions, just because you say so?

Forgiveness is a choice, a declaration. "I forgive myself. I'm sad and I regret what I did, but I forgive myself. I forgive myself just because I say so."

Sometimes you can release your guilt in an instant. That's how long you took to create it. Sometimes, releasing a guilt takes longer. Sometimes you need to forgive yourself over and over, until your guilt is finally gone.

If releasing a guilt seems difficult, you are probably avoiding some aspect of yourself. Find what the aspect is and let in the hurt of being this way. Then repeat the questions.

Do whatever you need to release your guilt. Forgive yourself for everything you have ever done from the time you were born until now. Work with each item of guilt until all your guilt is gone.

As you become free of guilt, you feel better about yourself and better about life. You also become much more able to live in the experience of love.

ACTION TO TAKE

◆ Notice how much you have suffered from your guilt. Have you been punished enough? Are you now willing to be free of your guilt?

◆ List everything you have ever done that you feel guilty about. Then use the questions in this chapter to release your guilt.

◆ Notice that you have always acted consistent with the state of mind and the way you saw life at the time. If you were wiser and more aware you would have been able to act differently, but you weren't.

◆ Notice that you have always done the best you could with the very limited equipment that you had at the time. Forgive yourself for not being wiser and more aware.

◆ Work with this chapter until you are totally free of all guilt.

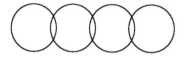

CHAPTER 12

LET GO OF RESENTMENT

Another way we sabotage ourselves is through resentment. When you have a resentment, a major part of you closes down. You lose your aliveness and your peace of mind. You become bitter and less able to express your love. You also make your life more difficult.

When you resent someone, you are saying, "I strongly dislike you." This destroys the experience of love. The other person then gets upset and becomes resentful toward you.

Then you get more upset and become more critical toward the other. Then the other person gets more resentful toward you. Soon you create a cycle of conflict that produces needless upset and suffering.

If you want to end the cycle of conflict and restore your peace of mind, you need to release your resentment.

Ironically, when you resent, you are the only one who really suffers. The other person is out enjoying life while you suffer with your upset.

Notice the price you pay for your resentment. Notice how much freedom, aliveness and peace of mind you have lost.

Letting go of a resentment is not for the benefit of the other person. Letting go of a resentment is for you. You release your resentment so you can heal your hurt and get on with your life.

We think that resentments are caused by other people, but they're not. No one has the power to create a resentment in you. Only you can do that.

You create your own resentment. You create resentment in a subconscious attempt to avoid your hurt.

Resentment is the forceful blaming of someone else. That person is the problem, the cause, the fault. Not you. You forcefully blame the other person so you don't have to look at yourself.

If you were to look at yourself, you would have to experience all the hurt from what happened. You would have to feel the hurt of being not good enough, not worth loving, or whatever your issue is. To avoid this hurt, you resent.

A good example of this took place several years ago. Karen resented Roger for leaving her. Under her anger and resentment, Karen had a deep hurt of feeling not worth loving. This was a hurt that she had spent most of her life avoiding.

When Roger left, this hurt was reactivated. His leaving proved that she wasn't worth loving. To avoid this hurt, Karen had to blame Roger for what had happened.

She couldn't dare face the possibility that Roger had left because she had been the problem. Karen was in turmoil because of her resentment and the suppressed feelings of being not worth loving.

When Karen came to see me, she faced her hurt and made peace with the aspect of her called not worth loving. Once this happened, she no longer needed her resentment. She forgave Roger and set herself free inside. She restored her peace of mind.

You can do the same thing. The process for releasing resentments is very simple. The process is similar to that of releasing guilt.

Be willing to feel the hurt that you've been avoiding and know that the other person is doing the best he or she can with that person's extremely limited equipment.

The moment you release your resentment, you physically feel the return of your aliveness. You restore the experience of love and your peace of mind.

If you have a resentment that you would like to be free of, you can use the following questions to let it go.

◆ Find the hurt that's under your resentment. Are you willing to feel this hurt?

◆ What do your circumstances say about

you? Do they say that you are not good enough or not worth loving? Find the words that hurt the most.

◆ Do you see that you are that way, that this is an aspect of you? Use the previous chapters to make peace with this aspect of yourself.

◆ Are you willing to feel the hurt of being this way? Are you willing to feel the hurt of what happened? Cry if you can.

◆ Are you willing to be free of your resentment? Have you suffered enough?

◆ Take a good look at the person you resent. Doesn't this person have a very particular state of mind and a very particular way of seeing life?

◆ Doesn't this person act totally consistent with his or her limited equipment?

◆ If the person was wiser and more aware, wouldn't the person be able to interact very differently?

◆ Do you see that the person isn't wiser and more aware? Do you see that the person has a very limited awareness?

◆ Are you willing to forgive the person for not knowing, for not being wiser and more aware?

◆ Doesn't this person do the very best he or she can with his or her limited equipment?

◆ Are you willing to forgive the person for acting consistent with his or her limited awareness?

◆ Are you willing to forgive the person for the damage that was done as a result of this limited awareness?

◆ Do you now totally forgive the person for not having been wiser and more aware, for acting consistent with his or her limited equipment, and for all the damage that the person has caused?

◆ Do you now let go of all resentment for the person, just because you say so?

Every time you release a resentment, you become more free inside. You restore your aliveness and your peace of mind. You restore your compassion and your ability to love.

If you have trouble releasing a resentment, look for what you are avoiding. What would you have to experience if you could no longer blame the person? Find what you are avoiding and be willing to experience it.

If releasing a resentment is still difficult, you may need to forgive by your declaration. "I hereby release all resentment for the person. I forgive, just because I say so." You may need to do this over and over.

List all of your resentments and do whatever it takes to release each one. The quality of your life depends on it.

ACTION TO TAKE

◆ Notice how much you have suffered from your resentment. Has your resentment changed anything? Are you now willing to be free of your resentment?

◆ List every resentment that you have. Then use the questions to release each one.

◆ Be willing to feel all the hurt from what happened. Find the aspects of you that you have been avoiding. Then make peace with them.

◆ Notice that the people you resent did the very best they could with their very limited equipment. Forgive each person for not being wiser and more aware.

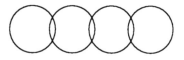

CHAPTER 13

MAKE PEACE WITH YOUR PARENTS

Most of us have a painful relationship with one or both of our parents. If this is true in your life, this is probably where you developed your hurt of feeling not okay.

Your parents implied, through their words and actions, that you were worthless, no good or whatever your issue is. To avoid this hurt, and to avoid facing this aspect of you, you put up your walls of protection.

You then became critical and resentful toward your parents. Then your parents got hurt. They put up their walls of protection and became even more non-accepting toward you. Then you got hurt even more.

Without knowing, you created a cycle of conflict that destroyed the experience of love, created more hurt and reinforced the feelings of being not okay.

To heal your relationship with your parents and to heal your hurt, you need to stop resisting your parents and make peace with the way that they are. You also need to make peace with any non-acceptance they have toward you.

You do this by making peace with the aspects of you that your parents reactivate. Avoiding these aspects is what causes you to resist.

Once you make peace with these aspects, the need to resist disappears. You can then end the conflict, heal your hurt and restore the experience of love in your relationship.

Now that you have worked with your issue and know about releasing resentment, you have the tools to make this happen.

Use the following steps to make peace with each of your parents. Do this exercise with one parent at a time. You can also use this exercise to make peace with other people, but do this with your parents first.

1. Discover the aspects of you that are being reactivated.

What did your circumstances say about you? How do you feel at the notion that every negative thing this person said or implied about you was the truth? How do you feel at the notion that you really are this way?

If this is a painful thought, or if you deny that this is true, you have found the nerve that creates your hurt and sabotages your relationship.

2. Realize that you are this way.

Let in the hurt of being this way. Cry if you can. Then use the steps in Chapter 9 to make peace with this aspect of you. Look for evidence to prove that you are this way.

Remember that being this way is irrelevant. It doesn't mean a thing. You are also the opposite.

3. Accept this person the way he or she is.

Notice that this person has a very particular state of mind and a very particular way of seeing life. This individual is the way he or she is whether you like it or not.

Let go of your demands for how you believe this person should be and make peace with the way he or she is. "I give you full permission to be the way you are."

4. Let go of all your resentment.

Notice that this person is doing the very best he or she can with his or her very limited equipment. Be willing to feel your hurt and forgive the person for not being wiser and more aware.

Use the preceding chapter to release any resentment you may have. Work with this until all your resentment is gone.

5. Find your role in the conflict.

Both of you are needed to create and maintain the cycle of conflict. Both of you are 100 percent responsible for the loss of love in your relationship. Find your 100 percent.

Notice how non-accepting and resentful you've been. Notice how you've destroyed the experience of love and how you've hurt this person.

Remember, you did the best you could with the limited equipment that you had at the time. Forgive yourself for any damage that you caused.

6. See that you are just like this person.

Notice that whatever you resist in this person is an aspect of you. You are just like this person. You may not do the same things, but these aspects are certainly in you.

If this is an uncomfortable thought, or if you deny that this is true, you have found another aspect that you've been resisting. Keep working with this until you see very clearly that this is an aspect of you.

Once you see that you are just like this person, your resistance disappears and is replaced with compassion. Until you see that you are the same way, you will continue to resist and your relationship will continue to suffer.

7. Communicate your hurt and express your love.

After you make peace with the way someone is, the next step is to get with that individual and clean up your relationship. Do this in person, by telephone or by letter.

Tell the person that your relationship is important and that you want to restore the love. Accept responsibility for the conflict and ask to be forgiven. Then tell the person of your hurt, but do so without blaming. Make sure the person feels loved, accepted and appreciated.

The purpose of this conversation is to restore the love, remove the distance and to shift the way the two of you interact with each other. Do whatever you can to make this happen.

For more information on healing relation-ships, read my book, *How To Heal A Painful Relationship.* My other book, *Miracles Are Guaranteed,* shows how to clean up your life.

Once you heal your relationship, you restore the experience of love. You heal more of your hurt and you become more at peace with you.

ACTION TO TAKE

◆ Use the steps in this chapter to make peace with your parents. This is important because in order to do this, you need to heal your hurt.

◆ Find the aspects of you that your parents reactivate and allow yourself to feel the hurt of being this way.

◆ Notice that your parents did the best they could with their limited equipment. Accept them for being the way they are and forgive them for not being wiser and more aware.

◆ Tell your parents that you want to restore the love. Take responsibility for the conflict and ask them to forgive you. Tell them of your hurt and tell them of your love.

◆ Use this chapter to make peace with anyone that you are resisting.

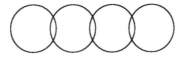

CHAPTER 14

ALLOW YOURSELF TO BE HUMAN

You are both good and bad, worthy and worthless, lovable and unlovable. You are every aspect that exists. You are also a precious human being.

Unfortunately, you lost the experience of your preciousness. You bought the notion that you are not okay and lost sight of who you are.

To see this more clearly, look at the little girl who got yelled at for being stupid.

If you were to see the girl, what would you think of her? Would you see her as stupid or would you see her as precious? Of course, you would see her as precious. To say that the little girl is stupid would be nonsense.

The little girl is precious. This is obvious to you and to me, but not to her. The moment she bought the notion that she was stupid, she started resisting herself and could no longer see how special she is.

The same thing happened to you. You got hurt and bought the notion that you weren't okay. Instantly, you became critical of yourself and lost the experience of your own preciousness. You are precious, but like the little girl, you can't see it.

Here is an exercise you can do to get the experience back. To get the best results, have someone walk you through the steps or use a tape recorder and play them back. This exercise is a very important step in the healing process. Make sure you take the time to do it.

◆ Close your eyes and get into a comfortable position.

◆ Take a deep breath and allow yourself to relax.

◆ Now imagine yourself as a child. See yourself with all the aspects that you've been resisting.

◆ Take a good look at this child. Isn't this child precious? Isn't this little person absolutely wonderful, adorable and lovable, just the way he or she is?

◆ Isn't this true even though all the aspects that you've been resisting are there?

◆ Now take a good look at this preciousness. Isn't it totally separate and distinct from whatever aspects you have? Isn't this preciousness the essence of who you are?

◆ Now bring in the grown child. Isn't this grown person also precious? Isn't this person also wonderful, adorable and lovable, just the way he or she is?

◆ Now get with the little child. Tell the child how sorry you are for having been so judgmental and critical of him or her.

◆ Ask the child to forgive you. Then listen to

whatever he or she has to say.

◆ Spend some time visiting with yourself as the child. Make sure both of you say whatever you need to heal your relationship and to fall back in love with each other. Take your time.

◆ When you are finished, give each other a big hug and then, when you are ready, open your eyes.

Something very special happens when you make peace with yourself. You fall back in love with you.

Do this exercise with yourself at each age that has been significant in your life. This can make a major difference in your relationship with you.

To fully experience who you are and to feel really good about yourself, you need to own every aspect of you. This includes not only the aspects that you consider negative, but also the ones that you consider positive.

So far, we have only been looking at the negative aspects. Now it's time to own the positive ones. Often, this is more difficult than owning the negative ones.

The first step in owning your positive aspects is to discover what they are. Make a list of everything you like about yourself. List all your talents, your abilities and your accomplishments. List every positive aspect of you that you can think of.

Making this list will have you look at yourself in a much more positive way.

When you finish, read the list to a friend. Be proud and read the list boldly. Don't hold back. This may be embarrassing, but telling someone of your positive aspects is the best way to own them. They then become more real and more a part of your daily life.

When you can't talk about these aspects, you can't own them. Keep reading your list until you can own them all.

As you own both your negative and positive aspects, you become very confident and at peace with yourself. You also become very human.

This humanness is the key to your dreams. As you allow yourself to be human, your ego stands aside and you become an expression of love. Life then works for you instead of against you.

Unfortunately, we are afraid to be human. We think that if we allow ourselves to be human, people won't like us anymore. To be liked, we have to be worthy, successful or some other aspect.

Actually, this is exactly opposite the truth. You never love someone because the person is worthy, successful or any other aspect.

You love someone when the person allows him or herself to be human. When someone sheds a tear or allows him or herself to be vulnerable, this is what melts your heart.

In one of our workshops, people discover the aspects that they've been running from. As you watch people discover their issues, two things happen.

First, you look at someone and wonder how the person came up with his or her issue. "Stupid, that's nonsense." "Not good enough? Where did you come up with that?" You see very clearly that these issues have nothing to do with the truth.

Second, you fall madly in love with the person. As the person owns his or her issue, the person becomes so human, your heart melts. You feel safe, you feel loved and you become much more able to be yourself. You see so clearly the beauty that the person is.

You are this same beauty. As you own the aspects of you that you've been resisting, this beauty comes forth. You become humble. Your ego disappears and your walls of protection come down. You flow with life and you create love everywhere you go.

Life is so much easier when you know that it's okay to be human.

ACTION TO TAKE

◆ Use the inner child exercise to heal your relationship with you. Do this exercise with yourself at each age that has been significant in your life. This exercise is very important. Make sure you do it.

◆ Make a list of everything you like about yourself. List your talents, your abilities and your accomplishments. List everything you can think of. Then read the list to a friend. This exercise allows you to own your positive aspects.

◆ Notice that you never love someone because the person is good enough, successful, or worth loving. You love someone when the person allows him or herself to be human.

◆ Allow yourself to be human. The key to doing this is to own the aspects of you that you've been resisting. This allows you to be humble, which automatically creates the presence of love.

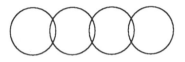

CHAPTER 15

TAKE ACTION

When you were little, you were pure love. You were happy, alive and free. You were fearless, creative and could flow with almost anything. Life was an exciting adventure.

Then you got hurt and started closing down. You bought the notion that you weren't okay and that you needed to be different than you were. Instantly, you lost your ability to be human.

You then spent the rest of your life avoiding this hurt, trying to become a certain way. In the process, you pushed away love and created your own fear, upset and suffering.

Now you have an opportunity to reverse the process.

You can heal your hurt and set yourself free inside. As you do this, you restore the love that you are. You become more human and more able to create a life that works.

To heal your hurt, you need to take away the resistance that creates it. You need to discover and make peace with the aspects of you that you've been resisting.

Use this book to make peace with as many aspects of you as you can. Then go through life looking for more. Look for upsets and look for any area of your life where you can't flow.

Whenever you can't flow with something, some hurt in you is being reactivated. To find what the hurt is, ask yourself, "What do those circumstances say about me?"

Find the aspects of you that you've been resisting and make peace with them. Every time you make peace with another aspect, you become more at peace with you and more able to flow with life.

Once you heal a particular hurt, the same circumstances can happen again and you won't get upset. You will see your situation clearly and can find solutions you could never have seen before.

As time goes on, the upsets in your life become fewer and fewer. Life becomes more enjoyable and more of your dreams come true.

The process for setting yourself free inside is relatively simple, but it doesn't happen by itself. You need to take some action. Make healing your hurt a top priority.

Life is too short to have it be anything less than a joy.

Thank you and
I love you.

Bill Ferguson

This is a book you will want to read over and over again. Each time you read it, you will heal more of your hurt and you will be more effective in life.

If you want to learn more about how to be free inside and how to have your life work, attend our programs, read our books and listen to our tapes.

You may want to have a telephone consulting session with Bill Ferguson or a member of his staff. If you are interested, call us at (713) 520-5370.

You can also find us on the internet at http://www.billferguson.com.

HOW TO HEAL A PAINFUL RELATIONSHIP

*And If Necessary,
How To Part
As Friends*

**This book is also available
on audio cassettes.**

Paperback, 156 pages

In this unique book,
Bill Ferguson shows,
step-by-step, how to remove
conflict and restore love in any
relationship. You will learn what creates
love and what destroys it. You will discover how
to end the cycle of conflict, heal hurt, release
resentment and restore your peace of mind. Bill's
experience as a former divorce attorney provides
rare insight into the nature of relationships. You
will discover something about yourself and your
relationships that will change your life forever.

ISBN 1-878410-25-3   Paperback $12
ISBN 1-878410-24-5   Two Audio Cassettes $16

MIRACLES ARE GUARANTEED

A Step-By-Step Guide To Restoring Love, Being Free And Creating A Life That Works.

Paperback, 160 pages

This book shows, step-by-step, how to have love in every aspect of your life. You will learn how to find and heal the issues that run your life and sabotage your dreams. You will learn how to take charge of your life and be free of upset and stress. You will discover how to clean up your life, find your life purpose and experience your spirituality. This profound yet simple book covers every aspect of living in the light.

ISBN 1-878410-20-2 Paperback $11

HEAL THE HURT THAT RUNS YOUR LIFE

Discover And Heal The Inner Issues That Destroy Love And Sabotage Your Life

This book is also available on audio cassettes.

Paperback, 120 pages

Every one of us has an inner issue that destroys love and sabotages life. What is your issue? Is it failure, not good enough or not worth loving? As you discover and heal this hurt, you profoundly change the way you live your life. Fear and upset seem to disappear. You become free inside and able to see life clearly. You become creative and far more effective. This life-changing book will show you how to find and heal this hurt.

ISBN 1-878410-21-0   Paperback $10
ISBN 1-878410-22-9   Two Audio Cassettes $16

THESE AUDIO CASSETTES WILL HELP YOU DISCOVER MORE ABOUT YOU, YOUR RELATIONSHIPS AND YOUR LIFE.

Set yourself free & enjoy your life

This album includes each of the following 8 audio cassettes for only $65.

Individual cassettes are available for $10.

ISBN 1-878410-01-6 $65

How To Love Yourself

- Be free of self-invalidation.
- Release the issues that run your life.
- Love yourself just the way you are.

ISBN 1-878410-02-4 $10

How To Have Love In Your Life

- Discover what creates love.
- Learn how to communicate effectively.
- Have love in all your relationships.

ISBN 1-878410-03-2 $10

How To Be Free Of Guilt And Resentments

- Be free of all anger, resentment and guilt.
- Restore your inner peace.
- Have difficult relationships work.

ISBN 1-878410-04-0 $10

How To Be Free Of Upset and Stress

- Be at peace in any circumstance.
- Release the mechanisms that keep you upset.
- Restore your piece of mind.

ISBN 1-878410-05-9 $10

How To Create Prosperity

- Release the mechanism that creates lack and financial stress.
- Remove your blocks to prosperity.
- Learn how to create abundance.

ISBN 1-878410-06-7 $10

How To Create A Life That Works

- Discover how you create your own unworkability.
- Be free of the hidden actions that sabotage you.
- Learn how to clean up your life.

ISBN 1-878410-07-5 $10

How To Find Your Purpose

- Earn a living doing what you love.
- Have your life make a difference.
- Discover your life purpose.

ISBN 1-878410-08-3 $10

How To Experience Your Spirituality

- Connect with your life force.
- Experience being one with God.
- Discover the Light.

ISBN 1-878410-09-1 $10

SPIRITUALITY: TEACHINGS FROM A WORLD BEYOND

Two audio cassettes

Several years ago, some profound teachings were received through a form of meditation. Since then, thousands of people have had their lives deeply altered. Through these teachings, you will discover the essence of spirituality. You will exper-ience a oneness with God and will discover a truth that will profoundly alter your life.

ISBN 1-878410-11-3 $16

HOW TO DIVORCE AS FRIENDS

Four Audio Cassettes

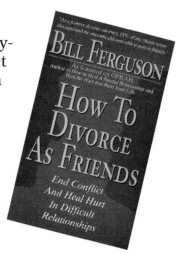

These tapes show, step-by-step, how to end conflict and restore cooperation in even the most difficult relationships. You will learn how to heal your hurt and be free of guilt and resentment. You will discover how to resolve issues quickly and effectively. You will learn how to part as friends.

Tape 1 - End The Cycle Of Conflict. Learn how to end conflict and restore your peace of mind.

Tape 2 - Heal Your Hurt. Find and heal the inner issues that create your pain and sabotage your life.

Tape 3 - Clean Up Your Relationship. Be free of guilt, anger, resentment and blaming.

Tape 4 - Resolve Issues Peacefully. Learn how to resolve your issues without conflict.

ISBN 1-878410-24-5   Four Audio Cassettes $25

TO ORDER BOOKS AND CASSETTES

Item		Price	Qty	Amount
Heal The Hurt That Runs Your Life	Book Audio	$10 $16		
How To Heal A Painful Relationship	Book	$10		
Miracles Are Guaranteed	Book	$11		
Set Yourself Free This album includes each of the following 8 audio cassettes		$65		
• How To Love Yourself	Audio	$10		
• How To Have Love In Your Life	Audio	$10		
• How To Be Free Of Guilt And Resentment	Audio	$10		
• How To Be Free Of Upset And Stress	Audio	$10		
• How To Create Prosperity	Audio	$10		
• How To Create A Life That Works	Audio	$10		
• How To Find Your Purpose	Audio	$10		
• How To Experience Your Spirituality	Audio	$10		
How To Divorce As Friends 2 Audio Cassettes		$16		
Spirituality: Teachings 2 Audio Cassettes		$16		
Subtotal				
Texas residents add 8% sales tax				
Shipping and handling: Add 10% of Subtotal $3 minimum, $6 maximum				
Total				

Name (Please print) _____

Address _____

City _____

State _____ Zip _____

Telephone Day ( )_____ Evening ( )_____

For MasterCard or Visa orders only:

Card No. _____ Total $_____

Exp. Date_____ Signature _____

Send your order along with your check or money order to:

Return to the Heart, P.O. Box 541813, Houston, Texas 77254
For Telephone orders Using MasterCard or Visa call (713) 520-5370
http://www.billferguson.com

If you want to have a telephone
consultation with Bill Ferguson or a member
of his staff, call us at
(713) 520-5370.

You can find us on the internet at
www.billferguson.com
www.divorceasfriends.com

TO ORDER BOOKS AND CASSETTES

Item		Price	Qty	Amount
How To Heal A Painful Relationship	Book Audio	$12 $16		
Heal The Hurt That Runs Your Life	Book Audio	$10 $16		
Miracles Are Guaranteed	Book	$11		
How To Divorce As Friends 4 Audio Cassettes		$25		
Set Yourself Free This album includes each of the following 8 audio cassettes		$65		
• How To Love Yourself	Audio	$10		
• How To Have Love In Your Life	Audio	$10		
• How To Be Free Of Guilt And Resentment	Audio	$10		
• How To Be Free Of Upset And Stress	Audio	$10		
• How To Create Prosperity	Audio	$10		
• How To Create A Life That Works	Audio	$10		
• How To Find Your Purpose	Audio	$10		
• How To Experience Your Spirituality	Audio	$10		
Spirituality: Teachings 2 Audio Cassettes		$16		
			Subtotal	
		Texas residents add 8% sales tax		
		Shipping and handling: Add 10% of Subtotal $4 minimum, $8 maximum		
			Total	

Name (Please print)_____

Address _____

City_____

State _____ Zip_____

Telephone Day (   )_____ Evening (   )_____

For MasterCard or Visa orders only:

Card No. _____ Total $_____

Exp. Date_____ Signature _____

Send your order along with your check or money order to:

Return to the Heart, P.O. Box 541813, Houston, Texas 77254
For Telephone orders Using MasterCard or Visa call (713) 520-5370
www.billferguson.com • www.divorceasfriends.com